McGraw-Hill Reading

Wonders

CCSS Reading/Language Arts Program

Program Authors

Diane August

Donald R. Bear

Janice A. Dole

Jana Echevarria

Douglas Fisher

David Francis

Vicki Gibson

Jan Hasbrouck

Margaret Kilgo

Jay McTighe

Scott G. Paris

Timothy Shanahan

Josefina V. Tinajero

Bothell, WA • Chicago, IL • Columbus, OH • New York, NY

Cover and Title Pages: Nathan Love

www.mheonline.com/readingwonders   C

The *McGraw·Hill* Companies

 Education

Copyright © 2014 by The McGraw-Hill Companies, Inc.

Send all inquiries to:
McGraw-Hill Education
Two Penn Plaza
New York, NY 10121

ISBN: 978-0-02-119721-7
MHID: 0-02-119721-0

Printed in the United States of America.

5 6 7 8 9 RMN 17 16 15 14

Unit 10 Thinking Outside the Box

The Big Idea: How can new ideas help us?

(t) Jo Parry; (c) Holli Conger; (b) SW Productions/Photodisc/Getty Images

Essential Question

What can happen when we work together?

Go Digital!

Teamwork!

Talk About It

How are these children working together?

5

u u_e
_ew _ue

Say the name of each picture.

1

2

Read each word.

3   **use**   **rule**   **cute**

4   **rude**   **tube**   **cube**

who	good

Who can use the paint?

You did a **good** job!

7

A Good Time for Luke!

Luke is five.

He can run quick.

We like to play with Luke.

Jo Parry

Set up a date for Luke!
Jot Luke a quick note.
We can have a **good** time.

We are here for Luke.
Deb can set it up, up, up!
Tim has a bit of tape to fix
a rip.

Mike can make a big cake.
He can make it in a tin pan.
June can use a red tube.

Look! June can tape it up
on top.
Luke can take it home.
Luke is a fun kid in luck!

Jo Parry

Who can get Luke?
Where can we hide?
Luke will like it a lot!

Luke can see Deb, Tim, Mike, June, and Kate. Luke can have fun. We have fun with Luke!

Jo Parry

Word Choice

Read Ruby's dialogue.

Ruby's model

"I made a huge sandwich. It tastes yummy!" said Ruby.

Pronouns

Pronouns take the place of nouns in a sentence.

Mom and I painted my room blue.

Celia has a little brother. He is funny.

17

Essential Question
In what ways are things alike?
How are they different?

Go Digital!

Talk About It
Why is it helpful
to sort things?

COLLABORATE

A Place for Everything

Say the name of each picture.

Read each word.

3	me	see	be	Eve
4	seed	fee	beet	Pete

come	**does**

We will **come** to New York.

Does this bus go north?

We Come on Time!

Holli Conger

We sit in a line.

It can take gas and time.

We do not need to be late.

Holli Conger

Jan and Pete can take
a bus.
Kim **does** not have to ride.
Kim does not see Pete.

Tom can ride a red bike.
He can go up, up, up.
But it is a quick ride to get
back home.

Dad has a job at a dock.
He can take Tim in a van.
Tim will not **come** late.

If it is wet, a van can help.
Dad can fit five in the van.
Dad can help a kid who
does not have a ride.

Holli Conger

If it is not wet, do not ride.

Lee and Kim can run,
run, run.

Pat can zip, zip quick, too!

Holli Conger

We come in at the
same time.
We get in and sit on time.
Pat can get in line quick!

Voice

Read Ella's thank-you note.

Ella's model

Dear Gran,
Thank you for the
green shirt!
Love, Ella

Pronouns

Pronouns take the place of nouns in a sentence.

Mom bought bean seeds. We can plant them.

It fills the sky with color!

Jenna Riggs

Essential Question
What ideas can you suggest
to protect the environment?

Go Digital!

Talk About It

How are these
children helping
to protect
our planet?

COLLABORATE

Save the Planet!

Review Letter Sounds

Say the name of each picture.

1

2

Read each word.

3   **cake   bone   kite   Pete**

4   **rope   use   ate   meet**

Review Words

Read the words and sentences.

1. **help**   **too**   **play**   **has**

2. **where**   **look**   **who**

3. **good**   **come**   **does**

---

4. **Does** Mike want to **help** , **too** ?

5. **Come** and **look** at my plant!

Who Can Help?

Dad **has** a big job.
He can do quite a lot.
Who can **help** Dad save
a lake?

Use a box, not a bag.
You can fit a lot in a box.
Yum, a kid can pack a
good box, **too** .

A mom can **come** and go.
It can take a lot of gas
to go.
But we save time and gas.

We can take a bus ride.
It can get us back home.
A bus can take a lot of us
where we like to go!

A kid can ride a bike.
It is fun to **play** like this.
It **does** not take gas to
ride, run, and hop.

A van can be a fun ride.
But it can use a lot of gas.
Look to see if five can fit
in the back!

See, a kid can do a lot!
A kid can fix. A kid
can save.
A little bit can help a lot.

Voice

Read Luke's poster.

Luke's model

I think you should turn off the tap to save water!

Jeff Hopkins

Pronouns

Pronouns take the place of nouns in a sentence.

Dad and I rode to see Grandma.

The hawk was in the tree, and it saw me.

45